BAC 'LI...

R A F'S FIRST LEVEL S...
POWERED WITH TWO A...
'AVONS', MOUNTED ONE...
FUSELAGE. LEVEL FLIGH...
WITH HIGH RATE OF CLIMB AND HIGH CEILING.
SPAN 34′ 10″. LENGTH 50′

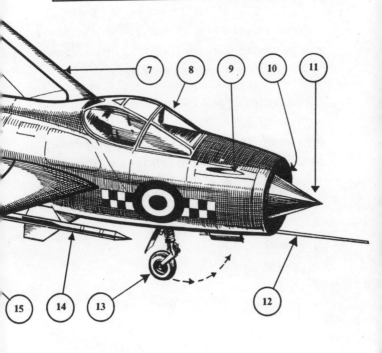

13 RETRACTABLE NOSE-WHEEL	**19** AILERON
14 FIRESTREAK MISSILE	**20** TRAILING EDGE
15 LEADING EDGE	**21** ELEVATOR
16 RETRACTABLE MAIN WHEEL	**22** TAILPLANE
17 STARBOARD MAINPLANE	**23** JET OUTLETS
18 NAVIGATION LIGHT	**24** RUDDER

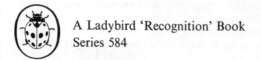

A Ladybird 'Recognition' Book
Series 584

Here is an exceptionally well-illustrated and inexpensive book that will be welcomed by aircraft enthusiasts of all ages.

Illustrated in full colour are 48 of the most interesting aircraft of various countries, from the small two-seater trainers to the huge passenger-carrying and military jet aircraft.

AIRCRAFT

by DAVID CAREY
with illustrations by B. KNIGHT

Publishers: Ladybird Books Ltd . Loughborough
© Ladybird Books Ltd (formerly Wills & Hepworth Ltd) 1972
Printed in England

Piper Pawnee B

The Piper company of America make several light cabin monoplanes, famous among which are the Comanche and Cherokee models. The Pawnee is also well known but is mainly used in agriculture for crop and field spraying. It is fitted with tanks which can deliver either liquid or powdered chemicals. A second, extra seat can be provided to carry a mechanic.

Make: American. *Engine:* 1 Lycoming six-cylinder, horizontally-opposed piston engine rated at 235 h.p. *Cruising speed:* 100 m.p.h. *Range:* 300 miles. *Wing span:* 36 feet 2 inches. *Length:* 24 feet 7 inches.

Britten-Norman Islander BN-2A

A general purpose light aeroplane, the Islander can carry a crew of one or two and up to ten passengers. It may also be used as a flying ambulance in which role it carries two stretcher cases and two attendants in addition to the crew. This machine is also assembled in Rumania from British-made parts.

Make: British. *Engines:* 2 Lycoming six-cylinder, horizontally-opposed piston engines each rated at 260 h.p. *Cruising speed:* 155 m.p.h. at 9,500 feet. *Maximum range:* 810 miles. *Wing span:* 49 feet. *Length:* 35 feet 7$\frac{3}{4}$ inches.

4

0 7214 0331 X

Auster Aiglet

This light monoplane is a two/three-seater training or touring machine. It is able to take off and land in quite small fields, and is very manœuvrable in flight. There are several other versions of the Auster, both civilian and military, and among these the Air Observation Post military aircraft and agricultural crop sprayers are perhaps the best known.

Make: British. *Engine:* 1 de Havilland Gipsy Major giving 130 h.p. *Cruising speed:* 112 m.p.h. *Maximum range:* 270 miles. *Wing span:* 32 feet. *Length:* 23 feet 5 inches.

Hawker Siddeley Gnat T.1

Called the Gnat chiefly because it is smaller and lighter than most modern jet aircraft, this aeroplane is in general use to train pilots for the R.A.F. It has been developed from the Gnat single-seat fighter-bomber, numbers of which are still serving with various overseas air forces, particularly in India where it is still being built under licence.

Make: British. *Engine:* 1 Bristol Siddeley Orpheus turbojet of 4,230 lb. static thrust. *Maximum speed:* 636 m.p.h. at 31,000 feet. *Maximum flying time:* $2\frac{1}{4}$ hours. *Wing span:* 24 feet. *Length:* 31 feet 9 inches.

BAC 167 Strikemaster

Similar in general design to the Jet Provost described in a previous edition of this book, the Strikemaster is a two-seat, side-by-side trainer and light fighter or counterattack aircraft. In its fighting role, it can be armed with two machine guns, an impressive load of rockets or four 500-lb. bombs. It is used by several Middle East air forces.

Make: British. *Engine:* 1 Rolls-Royce Bristol Viper turbojet of 3,410 lb. static thrust. *Maximum speed:* 480 m.p.h. at 20,000 feet. *Maximum range:* (operational) 600 miles. *Wing span:* 35 feet 4 inches. *Length:* 33 feet 7½ inches.

Canadair CL-215

Here is a multi-purpose amphibian which can land on water like a flying-boat, or on land with its retractable wheels lowered. It was originally developed for the water-bombing of forest fires in Canada and is used in France and Spain for the same purpose. As a passenger-carrier it will accommodate nineteen people on folding canvas seats.

Make: Canadian. *Engines:* 2 Pratt & Whitney radial, air-cooled piston engines each of 2,100 h.p. *Maximum cruising speed:* 190 m.p.h. at 8,000 feet. *Range:* 350 to 1,250 miles, depending on load. *Wing span:* 93 feet 10 inches. *Length:* 63 feet 6½ inches.

Hawker Siddeley Harrier

A single-seat strike and reconnaissance fighter in service with the R.A.F. and capable of carrying a variety of armament. It is a V/STOL (Vertical or Short Take-off and Landing) aircraft in which the turbofan engine can be swivelled, or vectored, to give vertical, angled or forward thrust. It can take off and land in very small spaces.

Make: British. *Engine:* 1 Rolls-Royce Bristol Pegasus vectored-thrust turbofan of 19,200 lb. static thrust. *Maximum speed:* (with typical load) 660 m.p.h. at 1,000 feet. *Rate of climb:* 10,000 feet in 40 sec. *Wing span:* 25 feet 3 inches. *Length:* 46 feet 4 inches.

BAC/Breguet Jaguar

The Jaguar is a joint product of the British BAC and French Breguet companies. It is made in single-seat fighter and two-seat advanced trainer versions, the fighter being able to carry a missile load of up to 10,000 lb. The first of these aircraft entered service with the French air force during 1971 and deliveries to the R.A.F. are due to commence in 1972.

Make: British and French. *Engines:* 2 Rolls-Royce-Turbomeca turbofans each of 4,600 lb. static thrust. *Maximum speed:* 1,130 m.p.h. at 33,000 feet. *Range:* (on typical operational mission) 775 miles. *Wing span:* 27 feet 10½ inches. *Length:* 50 feet 11 inches.

Westland Scout

This is a five-seat, light, general-purpose and reconnaissance helicopter. It is mainly used by the British Army but some have been supplied to the Royal Australian Navy for survey work, the Bahrein State Police, Uganda Police and the Jordanian Army. A similar machine, the Wasp, is being supplied to South Africa.

Make: British. *Engine:* 1 Rolls-Royce Bristol Nimbus turboshaft of 685 s.h.p. *Cruising speed:* 122 m.p.h. *Range:* 322 miles. *Rotor diameter:* 32 feet 3 inches. *Length (fuselage):* 30 feet 7½ inches.

Westland Sea King

A British version of the American Sikorsky SH-3D Sea King helicopter, the Westland Sea King is an amphibious anti-submarine warfare machine. It is being supplied to the Royal Navy mainly for its primary anti-submarine role but also for air-to-surface strike missions, search-and-rescue operations, troop transport, casualty lifting and cargo carrying.

Make: British (under U.S. licence). *Engines:* 2 Rolls-Royce Bristol Gnome turboshafts each of 1,500 s.h.p. *Cruising speed:* 131 m.p.h. *Range:* 690 miles. *Rotor diameter:* 62 feet. *Length:* (fuselage) 54 feet 9 inches.

B.KNIGHT

Mikoyan MIG 21PF

Although it is not likely to be seen over Britain, this Russian single-seat fighter is sometimes in the news and its name, if not its shape, is quite familiar. This version is armed with one 30-m.m. gun and two homing anti-aircraft missiles (AAMs), or two pods each containing 16 55-m.m. rockets. It is in service with the Russian, East German, Chinese Communist and Middle East air forces.

Make: Russian. *Engine:* 1 Tumansky turbojet giving 10,000 lb. static thrust (13,200 lb. static thrust with afterburning). *Maximum speed:* 1,450 m.p.h. at 36,000 feet (2¼ times the speed of sound). *Wing span:* 25 feet. *Length:* 49 feet.

McDonnell Douglas Phantom F.G.R. Mk. 2

Depending on the version, this two-seat, fighter aircraft can be operated from an aircraft carrier or from the land. It has been in service with the various United States air forces for some years and is now in operation with the R.A.F. and Royal Navy. It can carry a variety of armament according to operational requirements.

Make: American. *Engines:* 2 Rolls-Royce Spey turbo-fans each of 12,250 lb. static thrust (20,515 lb. with afterburning). *Maximum speed:* 1,386 m.p.h. at 40,000 feet. *Initial rate of climb:* 32,000 ft/min. *Wing span:* 38 feet 4¾ inches. *Length:* 57 feet 11 inches.

Handley Page Jetstream 3M

The Jetstream is a light executive and general transport plane which will carry a normal crew of two and between eight and twelve passengers according to cabin layout. It is in use mainly by private companies for air charter work and for carrying business-men quickly on cross country journeys. A Jetstream 2 with different power units is also in production.

Make: British. *Engines:* 2 Garrett AiResearch turbo-props each of 840 s.h.p. *Maximum cruising speed:* 288 m.p.h. at 15,000 feet. *Range:* (with 12 passengers and fuel reserves) 950 miles. *Wing span:* 52 feet. *Length:* 47 feet 1½ inches.

Hawker Siddeley HS 125 Series 400

The HS 125 is another type of executive aircraft from the Hawker Siddeley Group. Its normal accommodation provides for a crew of two and six passengers but it can carry up to twelve passengers with different seating arrangements. Another version of this aeroplane, known as the Dominie T, is used by the R.A.F. as a navigational trainer.

Make: British. *Engines:* 2 Rolls-Royce Bristol turbojets each of 3,360 lb. static thrust. *Normal cruising speed:* 450 m.p.h. at 40,000 feet. *Range:* 1,700–1,900 miles. *Wing span:* 47 feet. *Length:* 47 feet 5 inches.

Dassault Mirage III E

A single-seat strike fighter from France with a performance similar to that of the American Phantom, the Mirage is operated by the air forces of France, Israel, South Africa, Australia and Switzerland. It is armed with two 30-m.m. cannon and three AAMs (air-to-air missiles). Alternatively it can carry an 8,800 lb. load of bombs.

Make: French. *Engine:* 1 SNECMA Atar turbojet of 9,436 lb. static thrust (13,624 lb. with afterburning). *Maximum speed:* 1,386 m.p.h. at 40,000 feet. *Operating range:* (normal fuel) 180 miles. *Wing span:* 26 feet 11½ inches. *Length:* 46 feet 2½ inches.

BAC Lightning

The Lightning has generally taken the place of the Hawker Hunter in R.A.F. Fighter Command. It is a single-seat, all-weather interceptor armed with two or four 30-m.m. cannon and two Firestreak missiles, or forty-four 2-in. rockets. It can fly at just over twice the speed of sound, and has an exceptional rate of climb.

Make: British. *Engines:* 2 Rolls-Royce Avon turbojets each giving 12,690 lb. static thrust (16,360 lb. with afterburning). *Approximate maximum speed:* 1,500 m.p.h. at 40,000 feet. *Maximum climbing rate:* 50,000 feet per minute. *Wing span:* 34 feet 10 inches. *Length:* 50 feet.

Lockheed F-104S Starfighter

Probably one of the most widely used single-seat fighters in the world, the Starfighter is in service with many air forces. Although of American origin it is also built in Europe, Japan and Canada. Armament normally consists of one 20-m.m. rotary cannon and a variety of missiles up to a maximum load of 4,000 lb.

Make: American. *Engine:* 1 General Electric turbojet of 17,900 lb. static thrust with afterburning. *Maximum speed:* 1,450 m.p.h. at 40,000 feet. *Maximum rate of climb:* 50,000 ft/min. *Wing span:* 21 feet 11 inches. *Length:* 54 feet 9 inches.

Short Skyvan Series 3

A very different type of aeroplane is this Utility Transport. It has a crew of two and can carry a variety of loads, including up to eighteen passengers, twelve stretchers with attendants, or vehicles and agricultural equipment up to a limit of four thousand six hundred pounds. A large rear loading door is provided.

Make: British. *Engines:* 2 Garrett AiResearch turbo-props each of 757 e.s.h.p. *Normal cruising speed:* 170 m.p.h. at 10,000 feet. *Range:* 190–777 miles depending on load. *Wing span:* 63 feet 11 inches. *Length:* 40 feet 1 inch.

McDonnell Douglas Skyhawk

A single-seat, shipboard attack bomber, the Skyhawk has been supplied to Israel as well as to the Australian and U.S. navies and the New Zealand air force. As a carrier-based aircraft it carries two 20-m.m. cannon and an 8,200 lb. bomb and missile load. This load can be increased to nearly 12,000 lb. for shore-based operations.

Make: American. *Engine:* 1 Pratt & Whitney turbojet of 9,300 lb. static thrust. *Maximum speed:* 675 m.p.h. at sea level. *Range:* (on typical mission) 380 miles. *Wing span:* 27 feet 6 inches. *Length:* 42 feet 10¾ inches.

VFW-Fokker VFW 614

Built in collaboration between Federal Germany, Holland and Belgium, this aircraft is due to begin commercial operations in 1972/73 and has been ordered by several airlines. It is a short-haul transport with a crew of two and seating arrangements for 36 to 44 passengers. An unusual feature is the mounting of the engines above the wings.

Make: Germany. *Engines:* 2 Rolls-Royce/SNECMA turbofans each of 7,700 lb. static thrust. *Maximum cruising speed:* 457 m.p.h. at 21,000 feet. *Range:* (with 40 passengers) 715 miles. *Wing span:* 70 feet 6½ inches. *Length:* 67 feet 5¾ inches.

Hawker Siddeley Buccaneer

In regular service with the Royal Navy, the Buccaneer is a two-seat, shipboard, low-level strike aircraft that can carry nuclear or conventional weapons in the form of bombs, rockets and ASMs. A land-based version of the Buccaneer is in service with the South African Air Force as well as the R.A.F.

Make: British. *Engines:* 2 Rolls-Royce Spey turbofans each of 11,000 lb. static thrust. *Estimated maximum speed:* 700 m.p.h. at sea level. *Wing span:* 44 feet. *Length:* 63 feet 5 inches.

Breguet 1150 Atlantic

The Atlantic is a long-range, maritime patrol aircraft manufactured by French, Belgian, Dutch and German companies working in co-operation. It first entered service in 1966 and is at present flying with the German, Dutch, French and Italian air arms. It carries a crew of twelve and may be armed with homing torpedoes, depth charges or bombs, depending on its mission.

Make: French. *Engines:* 2 Rolls-Royce Tyne turboprops each of 6,105 e.h.p. *Long range cruising speed:* 311 m.p.h. at 26,250 feet. *Range:* (typical patrol) 620 miles plus time over target area. *Wing span:* 119 feet $1\frac{1}{4}$ inches. *Length:* 104 feet $1\frac{1}{2}$ inches.

Grumman Gulfstream II

Described as an Executive Transport but large enough to accommodate thirty passengers in a commercial transport role, the Gulfstream II is a jet development of an earlier turboprop aircraft. In its executive capacity it has a crew of three and various cabin arrangements to carry between ten and nineteen people. First flown on October 2nd, 1966.

Make: American. *Engines:* 2 Rolls-Royce Spey turbofans each of 11,400 lb. static thrust. *Normal cruising speed:* 496 m.p.h. at 40,000 feet. *Range:* 3,178 miles. *Wing span:* 68 feet 10 inches. *Length:* 79 feet 11 inches.

Nord 262 C

This is a light commercial transport plane with a range of only 405 miles in the fully-laden condition. It carries a crew of two and has accommodation for a maximum of 29 passengers. First flown in 1962, the 262 is in service with several operators including Japan Domestic Airlines, Air Ceylon and Air Madagascar as well as the French armed forces.

Make: French. *Engines:* 2 Turbomeca Bastan turboprops each of 1,140 s.h.p. *Maximum cruising speed:* 253 m.p.h. at 15,000 feet. *Range:* (29 passengers with luggage) 405 miles. *Wing span:* 74 feet $10\frac{1}{4}$ inches. *Length:* 63 feet 3 inches.

Lockheed Hercules (C-130 K)

The Hercules is a very successful and widely used aircraft of which well over a thousand have so far been built. It is a medium to long-range military transport with accommodation for 92 troops, 64 paratroops or 74 stretcher cases in addition to its crew of four. We illustrate the C-130 K model operated by the R.A.F., but other variations are in service.

Make: American. *Engines:* 4 Allison turboprops each of 4,500 e.s.h.p. *Maximum cruising speed:* 375 m.p.h. *Range:* (with maximum load) 2,450 miles. *Wing span:* 132 feet 7½ inches. *Length:* 99 feet 6 inches.

Fokker F.27 Friendship

Originally of Dutch manufacture, the F.27 Friendship is also built by the Fairchild Company of America and is powered by British engines. It is a short to medium-range commercial transport with accommodation for 52 to 56 passengers and is used by several airlines all over the world, including Aer Lingus of Ireland.

Make: Dutch. *Engines:* 2 Rolls-Royce Dart turboprops of 2,250 e.s.h.p. *Average cruising speed:* 291 m.p.h. at 20,000 feet. *Range:* 1,135 miles. *Wing span:* 95 feet 2 inches. *Length:* 82 feet 2½ inches.

B. KNIGHT

Transall C.160

A medium-range military transport, the Transall C.160 is a combined product of France and Germany, and is in service with the air forces of these two countries as well as the South African air force. It will carry 81 troops or 62 stretcher cases, or light armoured vehicles, tanks, etc.

Make: French and German. *Engines:* 2 Rolls-Royce Tyne turboprops each of 5,665 s.h.p. *Maximum cruising speed:* 332 m.p.h. at 14,800 feet. *Range:* (with maximum load) 1,070 miles. *Wing span:* 131 feet 2½ inches. *Length:* 105 feet 3½ inches.

Sud-Aviation Caravelle 12

One of the first aircraft to have its two jet engines mounted on either side of the fuselage at the rear, the Caravelle is a short to medium-range commercial airliner. It is operated by Air France as well as airlines throughout the world, and has accommodation for 89 passengers. There are various versions flying, with several engine alternatives.

Make: French. *Engines:* 2 Pratt & Whitney turbofans each giving 14,500 lb. static thrust. *Maximum cruising speed:* 500 m.p.h. at 25,000 feet. *Range:* 1700–2367 miles at 30,000 feet. *Wing span:* 112 feet 6½ inches. *Length:* 118 feet 10 inches.

Hawker Siddeley Trident 3B

So named because of its three rear-mounted jet engines, the Trident is one of Britain's most popular aircraft now in service. The latest version is designed to carry from 128–171 passengers over distances of up to 1,660 miles. First flown in January, 1962, the Trident is now operating with British European Airways, Pakistan International and certain Middle East airlines.

Make: British. *Engines:* 3 Rolls-Royce Spey turbofans each giving 11,930 lb. static thrust. *Maximum cruising speed:* 601 m.p.h. at 28,300 feet. *Wing span:* 98 feet. *Length:* 131 feet 2 inches.

Tupolev TU 134 A

This Russian short to medium haul commercial transport is in service with Russia's Aeroflot airline and several airlines in Eastern European countries. Like the French Caravelle, the two jet engines are mounted at the tail. Accommodation is provided for a crew of three and a maximum of 84 tourist-class passengers in four-abreast seats.

Make: Russian. *Engines:* 2 Soloviev turbofans each of 14,990 lb. static thrust. *Normal cruising speed:* 466 m.p.h. at 32,810 feet. *Normal range:* 1,242 miles. *Wing span:* 95 feet 2 inches. *Length:* 121 feet 8¾ inches.

Vickers (BAC) Viscount 810

Although no longer in production, the Viscount is still widely used by British European Airways and many overseas airlines, including Middle East Airlines, South African Airways and Trans Canada Airlines. Some were even ordered by the Chinese Republic. It is particularly useful for busy routes over fairly short distances. About five hundred Viscounts of all types were built. Accommodation is provided for 52 to 70 passengers.

Make: British. *Engines:* 4 Rolls-Royce Dart turboprops each giving 1,990 e.s.h.p. *Cruising speed:* 360 m.p.h. at 20,000 feet. *Wing span:* 93 feet $8\frac{1}{2}$ inches. *Length:* 85 feet 8 inches.

Hawker Siddeley 748

This is basically a short to medium-range commercial transport with various cabin arrangements to carry from 40 to 58 passengers. A military transport version, known as the Andover, is also built. This will carry 30 paratroops or 18 stretcher cases or a 10,500 lb. vehicle. Assembly also takes place in India for the Indian Air Force.

Make: British. *Engines:* 2 Rolls-Royce Dart turboprops each of 2,290 e.s.h.p. *Cruising speed:* 267 m.p.h. at 25,000 feet. *Range:* 1,957 miles (approx.). *Wing span:* 98 feet 6 inches. *Length:* 67 feet.

Lockheed TriStar

The TriStar is a new short to medium haul passenger transport from America scheduled to enter airline service late in 1971. Its early production programme was interrupted by financial troubles at Rolls-Royce whose RB 211 engine was specially designed to power it. Accommodation is provided for 279 passengers sitting eight-abreast or 330 nine-abreast passengers plus a crew of three or four.

Make: American. *Engines:* 3 Rolls-Royce RB 211 turbofans each of 40,600 lb. static thrust. *Average cruising speed:* 530 m.p.h. at 35,000 feet. *Range:* (with maximum load) 2,250 miles. *Wing span:* 155 feet 4 inches. *Length:* 177 feet 8 inches.

Hawker Siddeley Nimrod

A long-range, maritime patrol aircraft, the Nimrod carries a crew of eleven and an armament of homing torpedoes, depth charges and anti-submarine missiles. One of the R.A.F.'s latest aircraft, the Nimrod became operational in 1970 and generally replaces the piston-engined Shackleton which served in the same capacity for many years.

Make: British. *Engines:* 4 Rolls-Royce Spey turbojets each of 11,500 lb. static thrust. *Average cruising speed:* 450 m.p.h. at 30,000 feet. *Wing span:* 114 feet 10 inches. *Length:* 126 feet 9 inches.

B. KNIGHT

Hawker Siddeley Vulcan

One of Britain's famous 'V' bombers, the HS Vulcan is in regular service with Strike Command of the R.A.F. It is a delta wing, long-range, medium bomber capable of launching a ballistic missile or carrying various loads of nuclear or conventional bombs at very nearly the speed of sound. Production was completed in 1964.

Make: British. *Engines:* 4 Bristol Siddeley Olympus turbojets each giving 20,000 lb. static thrust. *Approximate maximum speed:* 645 m.p.h. at 40,000 feet. *Maximum range:* 4,750 miles. *Wing span:* 111 feet. *Length:* 99 feet 11 inches.

Aviation Traders ATL-98 Carvair

This is a popular transport aircraft in which holiday-makers to the continent may well travel. It has a crew of two or three and accommodation for eighty-five passengers, or five cars and twenty-two passengers. Among several operators it is used by Aer Lingus, Air Transport and British United Air Ferries.

Make: British. *Engines:* 4 Pratt & Whitney radial piston engines each of 1,450 h.p. *Normal cruising speed:* 207 m.p.h. at 10,000 feet. *Range:* (fully loaded) 2,300 miles. *Wing span:* 117 feet 7 inches. *Length:* 102 feet 7 inches.

Boeing 737-200

The 737 is the smallest of the Boeing range of airliners and is used for short to medium hauls, carrying between 63 and 113 passengers depending on cabin layout. It has been in service since the end of 1967 and is operated by the German Lufthansa airline as well as several others, particularly in America.

Make: American. *Engines:* 2 Pratt & Whitney turbofans each of 14,500 lb. static thrust. *Normal cruising speed:* 506 m.p.h. at 30,000 feet. *Range:* (fully loaded) 2,080 miles. *Wing span:* 93 feet. *Length:* 100 feet.

BAC One-Eleven, Series 500

The One-Eleven is a fairly short to medium-range commercial transport that is serving with some British and overseas airlines. It has a crew of two and a maximum capacity of 109 passengers. The Series 500 is the latest, largest and most powerful version and serves with B.E.A. as the Super One-Eleven.

Make: British. *Engines:* 2 Rolls-Royce Spey turbofans each of 12,460 lb. static thrust. *Maximum cruising speed:* 548 m.p.h. at 35,000 feet. *Range:* (full load) 1,850 miles. *Wing span:* 93 feet 6 inches. *Length:* 107 feet.

Boeing 727

This is Boeing's short to medium-range commercial transport, not to be confused with the smaller and less powerful 737 or the long-range 707. It is operated by several of the world's major airlines. It uses a crew of three and has various cabin arrangements to carry up to a maximum of 180 tourist-class passengers.

Make: American. *Engines:* 3 Pratt & Whitney turbofans each of 14,000 lb. static thrust. *Maximum cruising speed:* 592 m.p.h. at 18,000 feet. *Range:* (full load) 1,130 miles. *Wing span:* 108 feet. *Length:* 153 feet 2 inches.

Handley Page Victor B (S.R.) Mk. 2

Another of Britain's 'V' bombers, the Victor is a swept-wing jet aircraft. Although originally designed for the bombing role, the Victor is now used mainly for long-range reconnaissance and high-level maritime patrol. It carries photoflash canisters in the weapons bay and uses a variety of camera equipment. A built-in processing unit produces continuous film strips of the radar displays.

Make: British. *Engines:* 4 Rolls-Royce Conway turbojets each of 19,725 lb. static thrust. *Approximate maximum speed:* 630 m.p.h. at 50,000 feet. *Normal range:* 2,500 miles at 50,000 feet. *Wing span:* 120 feet. *Length:* 114 feet 11 inches.

McDonnell Douglas DC-9

Like the Boeing 727, the McDonnell Douglas DC-9 is one of America's popular short to medium-range commercial transport aircraft. It serves with over twenty airlines in many parts of the world, including several European operators. It can carry up to 90 tourist-class passengers plus a crew of two and cabin attendants.

Make: American. *Engines:* 2 Pratt & Whitney turbofans each of 14,500 lb. static thrust. *Cruising speed:* 560 m.p.h. at 25,000 feet. *Range:* 1,400–1,800 miles. *Wing span:* 93 feet $3\frac{1}{2}$ inches. *Length:* 104 feet $4\frac{3}{4}$ inches.

Ilyushin IL-62 (Classic)

A long-range airliner from Russia, the IL-62 is also known as the 'Classic'. It is in operation with the Aeroflot airline and first flew on its Moscow to Montreal service in 1967. As with most commercial aircraft, it has alternative cabin layouts and the IL-62 can carry between 115 first-class passengers and 186 in a more closely-packed arrangement.

Make: Russian. *Engines:* 4 Kuznetsov turbofans each of 23,150 lb. static thrust. *Normal cruising speed:* 516 m.p.h. at 36,000 feet. *Range:* (with maximum load) 5,000 miles. *Wing span:* 143 feet. *Length:* 174 feet $2\frac{1}{2}$ inches.

McDonnell Douglas DC-8

The various versions of this airliner are fitted with a variety of engines. The series 60 (illustrated) has American Pratt & Whitney power plants and is a long-range, intercontinental machine that will carry up to 251 passengers. It is in service with many of the major airlines and well over five hundred have been built.

Make: American. *Engines:* 4 Pratt & Whitney turbofans each giving 18,000 lb. static thrust. *Maximum cruising speed:* 500 m.p.h. at 30,000 feet. *Range:* approximately 6,000 miles. *Wing span:* 142 feet 5 inches. *Length:* 187 feet 4¾ inches.

Boeing 707

This fine all-jet airliner is in regular service with many of the world's largest airlines, including British Overseas Airways Corporation. It is an intercontinental transport carrying 131 to 189 passengers, depending on the seating arrangement. It can also be quickly converted to a cargo-carrying role.

Make: American. *Engines:* 4 Pratt & Whitney turbofans each giving 18,000 lb. static thrust. *Maximum cruising speed:* 607 m.p.h. at 25,000 feet. *Range:* (with maximum load) 4,235 miles. *Wing span:* 145 feet 8½ inches. *Length:* 152 feet 11 inches.

B. KNIGHT

Tupolev TU-144 (Charger)

Russia's equivalent to the British and French Concorde, the TU-144, was the first supersonic commercial airliner to fly (31st December, 1968). It is due to enter service with Aeroflot at the end of 1972. Normal layout provides accommodation for a crew of three and 100 passengers. A droopable nose section gives good pilot visibility for take-off and landing.

Make: Russian. *Engines:* 4 Kuznetsov turbofans each of 28,660 lb. static thrust (38,580 lb. s.t. with afterburning). *Maximum cruising speed:* 1,550 m.p.h. at 49,000–65,000 feet. *Maximum range:* 4,040 miles. *Wing span:* 75 feet $5\frac{1}{2}$ inches. *Length:* 196 feet $10\frac{1}{4}$ inches.

BAC VC.10

Another of Britain's fine aircraft is the VC.10, a long-range intercontinental airliner designed to carry 135 passengers. It flew for the first time on 29th June, 1962, and is still in regular service with British Overseas Airways and several other airlines. A larger, more powerful VC Super 10 is also in service. Fifty four of all types had been built when production ended in 1969.

Make: British. *Engines:* 4 Rolls-Royce Conway bypass turbojets each giving 21,000 lb. static thrust. *Cruising speed:* 580 m.p.h. at 25,000 feet. *Wing span:* 146 feet 2 inches. *Length:* 146 feet 2 inches.

B. KNIGHT

Boeing 747

Often referred to as the 'Jumbo Jet', this huge aircraft has accommodation for as many as 490 passengers in ten-abreast seating. First flown early in 1969 it is now in operation with Pan American Airlines, B.O.A.C. and several other companies. Other versions of the 747 with more powerful engines are in the course of development.

Make: American. *Engines:* 4 Pratt & Whitney turbofans each of 43,500 lb. static thrust. *Normal cruising speed:* 590 m.p.h. at 35,000 feet. *Average range:* 4,600 miles. *Wing span:* 195 feet 8 inches. *Length:* 231 feet 4 inches.

BAC/Sud-Aviation Concorde

The Concorde, like the Tupolev TU-144, is a long-range supersonic airliner. A combined British and French project, it was first flown over France on 2nd March, 1969, the British-built version following on 9th April. It has maximum seating for 144 passengers and is fitted with a droopable nose. Later models will have a longer fuselage and more powerful engines.

Make: British and French. *Engines:* 4 Rolls-Royce Bristol/SNECMA Olympus turbojets each of 32,825 lb. static thrust (37,420 lb. s.t. with afterburning). *Normal cruising speed:* (estimated) 1,350 m.p.h. at 55,000–65,000 feet. *Range:* (with maximum load) 4,020 miles. *Wing span:* 83 feet 10 inches. *Length:* 184 feet 2 inches.

INDEX OF AIRCRAFT